Slip into Sleeping

Slip into Sleeping

HANDBOOK FOR HOW TO GET A GOOD NIGHT'S SLEEP

CAROL CAFFEY

Limits of Liability and Disclaimer of Warranty

The author/publisher shall not be liable for your misuse of this material. This book is strictly for informational and educational purposes.

Warning – Disclaimer

The purpose of this book is to educate and entertain. It is distributed with the understanding that the publisher is not engaged in the dispensation of legal, psychological or any other professional advice. The content of each entry is the expression and opinion of its author and does not necessarily reflect the beliefs, practices or viewpoints of the publisher, its parent company or its affiliates. The publisher's choice to include any material within is not intended to express or imply any warranties or guarantees of any kind. The author and/or publisher do not guarantee that anyone following these techniques, suggestions, tips, ideas, or strategies will become successful. The author and/or publisher shall have neither liability nor responsibility to anyone with respect to any loss or damage caused, or alleged to be caused, directly or indirectly by the information contained in this book.

Contents

Introduction

IT IS ESTIMATED OVER HALF of the population does not always get adequate sleep at night. This represents a huge number of people who are struggling to have a good night's sleep. If only they could sleep well during the night, they could wake up feeling refreshed and focused, ready to meet the day.

This book was written so you can have a wonderful night of sleep easily, naturally, healthfully. As I share this rich and effective information with you, I am speaking in an authoritative manner as if I am telling someone exactly what to do and how to do it. And actually, I am—that someone is--myself! I am speaking firmly and directly because these things work.

For years, I have been gathering information and tips on how to sleep well at night. And as ideas would occur to me, I would add them to the treasure trove. Along with this, I have done a great deal of experimenting. And so, I am sharing with you the results of these experiences.

Having said that, this information is for educational purposes only. It is not intended to give medical advice, diagnosis or treatment. It is not a substitute for medical or professional care. Before you make any changes to your diet, supplement, medication, exercise or sleep regimens, check with your physician or integrative health practitioner. Clear these things with them first. I assume no responsibility for your use, misuse or nonuse of this information.

CHAPTER 1
Preparing the Body

"Time to start getting more sleep. This beautiful
physique needs royal treatment."

— ELIZABETH RUDNICK

PREPPING THE BODY FOR A good night of sleep begins long before bedtime. Everyone knows what it feels like to be sleep deprived because of tossing and turning in the night and having to do your best to function the next day anyway. What and when you eat and drink during the day and evening has a huge effect on the quality of sleep experienced during the night. Here are some things to consider to make sure you are getting your body ready for a good night's sleep.

COFFEE AND CHOCOLATE
Caffeine can interfere with your internal biological clock, the body's natural sleep/wake rhythm. Caffeine blocks adenosine, the built-in, sleep-inducing substance in your body. Ingesting caffeine too late in the day can make it difficult to get to sleep. It can break up your sleep, making it shallow and restless.

Depending on how sensitive you are to caffeine, make your last cup of coffee around noon or, at the latest, midafternoon. This includes other drinks containing caffeine, such as tea or energy drinks. The same boundaries may need to be applied to chocolate. Theobromine is the main ingredient in chocolate that can keep a person awake half the night if there is a sensitivity to it. Chocolate also contains caffeine.

NAPPING

If you are sleepy after lunch, it would be best to take a nap early in the afternoon. A late afternoon or evening nap would stand a good chance of interfering with going to sleep easily at bedtime.

A fifteen- or twenty-minute nap during the early afternoon most likely will not compromise your ability to get to sleep at night. If you sleep longer than twenty minutes, you may experience the deeper cycles of sleep and feel heavy and groggy when you awaken. Just keep the nap short.

WATER

To maintain a healthy body, it is important to stay hydrated. Seventy per cent of your body is water. The cells in your body need water in order to crank out the energy your body runs on. In a dehydrated state, toxins accumulate at the cellular level and can trigger disease. It takes water to cleanse the cells.

If you become dehydrated in the night because you did not drink enough water during the day, you may find yourself waking up at night and getting up to get a drink of water so you can get back to sleep.

It is helpful for the purpose of sleep to drink most of the water you are going to consume in a given day before evening arrives. Make that purified water, please. Balancing the bulk of your water intake toward the daytime hours can eliminate or greatly cut down on trips to the bathroom during the night.

TIMING FOR DINNER

Dinner should be finished three hours before bedtime. That last meal of the day needs to be substantial enough so you are not hungry at bedtime. It is best to eat nothing and drink little during the three hours between dinner and bedtime.

If you have eaten dinner early in the evening and you find you are hungry by midevening, say an hour or two before bedtime, eat fresh or frozen fruit. It will be much easier and quicker to digest than processed food and therefore less likely to interfere with sound sleep.

LATE EATING

Eating late in the evening or at bedtime can interfere with your sleep because when the body digests food, the metabolism has to rev up to do the job. Depending on when the food was eaten and how much was consumed, the process of digestive activity can make it challenging to get to sleep and can wake you up during the night.

EATING AT BEDTIME

If the time for sleep arrives and you are hungry and you realize you are not going to be able to sleep clear through the night without food, eat a banana. This fruit contains sleep supporting substances of calcium, magnesium, potassium, tryptophan and melatonin, among other good things. Tryptophan is the substance in turkey that can make you feel a little drowsy after eating a big serving of it. Eating a banana will also trigger production of feel good neurotransmitters and hormones. Because bananas contain digestive enzymes, having a banana at bedtime does not seem to interfere at all with sleep during the digestive process.

However, ingesting a banana right before going to bed would not be a good thing to do as a regular habit, in spite of the fact it can work well. Maybe it's OK to eat a banana at bedtime in a pinch, once in a while. On a regular basis though, it is best to go to bed with an empty stomach because the brain detoxes during sleep. If the stomach is in a digestive mode in the night, the detoxing cannot happen efficiently.

ALCOHOL

Drinks containing alcohol should be consumed during the day or early evening, but not within three hours before bedtime. Drinking alcoholic beverages approaching bedtime may seem to aid in dropping off to sleep, but it can most certainly interfere with staying asleep. You may find yourself in a light stage of sleep and waking during the night. This will rob you of the deep cycles of sleep needed for healthy and restorative slumber.

Alcohol is also dehydrating. If you consume alcohol too close to bedtime, you may find you are making unwelcome multiple trips to the bathroom during the night.

EXERCISING

Some research has shown that, for the purpose of sleeping well at night, whatever physical exercise is done should be carried out during the day. There is evidence afternoon may be best. For most people, exercising in the evening, especially close to bedtime, is not a helpful practice because it stimulates the body to produce cortisol and gears up the metabolism. Cortisol is known as the stress hormone and can interfere with sleep.

However, there is a small percentage of people who do just fine with evening exercising and still have a restful night of sleep. Maybe you already know which category you fall into. At any rate, a bit of experimenting would quickly let you know.

Exercise, at whatever time is optimal for you, is a big plus for the nighttime scene. The body is more likely to be ready to settle into sleep if there has been exercise during the day or early evening.

Besides being a major factor for a healthy physical body, moderate exercise is also an effective all-around stress reducer and reliever. Which one of us could greatly benefit from that! Our sleep time could, for sure.

CHAPTER 2

Preparing the Bedroom

"The way you prepare the bed, so shall you sleep."

— YIDDISH PROVERB

DEFINITION OF A BEDROOM: a room for a bed.

And that bed is best used only for sleeping and love making. No TV, no reading.

Once you are asleep, nothing much in the room matters except the bed, quiet, peacefulness, darkness, temperature, comfort. Add to that freedom from EMFs (electromagnetic frequencies).

Could we say then that a room designated for sleeping could be furnished and decorated quite simply? What is really needed but a bed? Not much.

LIGHTED DEVICES

All lighted electronic devices need to be removed from your bedroom. This includes TV, computer, laptop, tablet, cellphone, electronic games. The light and frequencies these devices emit do not support good sleep. If you use lighted devices in the evening, it can take longer to get to sleep, and you may get less sleep. If you feel you must have your cellphone in the room, it should be turned off or at least on airplane mode. Otherwise, have the cellphone as far away from you as possible.

Turn off the Wi-Fi at bedtime. This electronic device functions on microwave frequency. Microwave heats and cooks food. While Wi-Fi operates at a much lower level than a microwave oven, this frequency is not conducive to sleeping at night.

ELECTRICAL ITEMS

There should be as few electrical items in your bedroom as possible. The object is to not be sleeping in a shower of unhealthy electrical frequencies.

Do away with the electric blanket. If you have lamps, make sure they are at least three feet away from you. If a lamp is turned off but still plugged in, even then it is creating an electrical field.

Another way to eliminate electrical frequencies in your bedroom is to turn off the circuit breaker to the bedroom at bedtime.

BED

The comfort level of your bed is, of course, highly important. Ideally, it is giving you support without being overly firm.

If you are planning to purchase a new bed, consider getting a mattress made of natural, organic materials—latex, cotton or wool. Also, choosing a mattress free from flame retardants would be sleep supporting and healthy.

SHEETS AND COVERS

Go for 100% cotton sheets and pillowcases. For blankets or comforters, 100% cotton or wool would be tops. Linen or silk would work too. Organic would be the best.

Why organic? Organic sheets, pillowcases and bed covers would be toxin free. Chemical free sleeping is healthy sleeping.

PILLOWS

Finding the right size and shape of pillow for a good sleep is definitely an individual matter. Only trial and error can solve that choice.

One style of pillow that works well for back sleepers is a foam cervical pillow. It is molded to give support to the neck when a person is in a supine position. If you are a back sleeper, you might also find a regular type of pillow under the knees to be quite comfortable and therefore sleep promoting.

A foam cervical pillow can also work for a side sleeper if it is raised up higher by placing a small pillow or a large folded towel under it. Raising the cervical pillow will allow the side sleeper to have better alignment of the spine during sleep.

A second pillow is needed if you are a side sleeper. This pillow needs to be between your knees all night long. This takes stress off the joints at the hips and knees because there will be a more natural alignment of the legs during the night. How do you keep the pillow between the knees as you turn from side to side while you are sleeping? It's easy. The body seems to learn quickly that you expect it to keep the pillow in place all night long. And so, it happens.

If you are a side sleeper and if a second pillow is used, another possibility would be to make that one a body pillow. Not only would your legs be in a more natural configuration, but your arms would be in a more natural position as well. Some people find it very comforting to be sleeping with this kind of pillow. The length of a body pillow is usually 54".

QUIET

It almost goes without saying that you need just about absolute quiet for a good night of sleep. If there is noise outside your living quarters that you have no control over, use earplugs. But then, if you use an alarm clock, the sound of the alarm would need to be loud enough to wake you—even with earplugs on. Using a sunrise alarm might be a viable option.

DARKNESS

The bedroom needs to be very dark. The darker your bedroom is at night, the better. Any light in the bedroom at night disrupts the light/dark circadian rhythm of the body. Consider installing blackout curtains if you have outside sources of light filtering into your bedroom. The ideal level of darkness has been attained when you cannot see your hand held in front of your face.

If your bedroom situation is such that you cannot make the changes necessary for ultimate darkness, wear a sleep mask. A natural fabric like silk or cotton would be a good choice.

ALARM CLOCK

It is best to use a battery-operated alarm clock. If the clock you use is a plug-in type, place it as far away from your bed as you can.

If you use an alarm clock with a lighted face, turn the face of the clock away from your bed. If the face of the clock is especially brightly lighted, cover the clock. It is important to preserve the darkness of the bedroom.

If the awakening feature of the alarm you use is based on sound, it would be good if the sound is at a low level when it first goes off and then builds more and more in the next few seconds. It is jolting and unpleasant to be suddenly awakened in the morning with a loud sound.

Alarm clocks are available with features of both light and sound as awakening modalities. They are called sunrise alarm clocks, and they often come with a sounds of nature feature. When the alarm goes off, the light comes on, gradually getting brighter and brighter, mimicking the rising sun. You can also choose from various nature sounds to accompany the intensifying light. A gentle way of being awakened.

NIGHT LIGHT

For the purpose of maintaining sleep during the night, it is best to not turn on a light. If a light is on for only one instant, it will disrupt the natural sleep cycle. Except, orange light will not. Himalayan salt lamps emit an orange glow, so they are ideal as night lights for the hallway and bathroom. This product is available in lamp form and also as a wall type, plug-in night light.

If you need to have some light in your bedroom to get from the bed to the bathroom, use a flashlight with an orange light. You can easily create one by using a Transparent Color Connection Lighting Gel Filter Set. A set of this sort is available with five sheets--five different colors. Use the orange, red and pink ones. Using the clear glass or plastic protecting the bulb as a template, cut a circle from each colored plastic sheet, insert into the flashlight under that clear piece, and you are ready to go.

TEMPERATURE

It seems to be that a room temperature of 60 to 69 degrees is ideal for sleeping at night. This is a good temperature range for cool/cold weather. Summer sleeping may not need that low of a temperature. For instance, if a person is experiencing an environment of 78 degrees during the day in the warm/hot months, it might not be necessary to go into the sixties at night for really good sleep. A setting of 75 degrees might be just fine. Check it out for yourself.

SLEEP PARTNER

If you presently sleep with a mate or partner and your sleep is interrupted by that person shifting position in bed during sleep, getting up in the night or snoring, separate bedrooms would be an ideal direction to go. If this is not possible in your present place of residence, twin beds would be another solution.

It might be challenging to arrive at the point of being able to make the decision to part ways as a sleep team, to sleep separately during the night. After all, this person is the love of your life. But could it be that love is fueling the decision? Not only will you be sleeping more soundly, your partner will as well. This way, both of you have a better chance of waking up feeling rested and refreshed, functioning wonderfully and in a good mood.

PETS

If you have pets, it would be best for optimal sleeping at night to situate them in another part of your living space, not in your bedroom. Your pets do not have the same sleep needs as yours. They do not have the same internal sleep/wake cycle as humans. Pets have more acute hearing than you do, and they tend to respond immediately to an unexpected sound.

You may be thinking, "Oh no, I can't be without my pets." But how much do you want an uninterrupted, undisturbed night of sleep? Might be worth it.

CHAPTER 3

Preparing Your Brain and Mind

"I have realized that most of my best ideas
have followed a good night's sleep."

— THOMAS EDISON

HUMAN BODIES HAVE A NATURAL, built in, 24-hour rhythm of light and dark called circadian rhythm. Before electricity, people were more in tune with this inner clock than they are now. When it got dark, they headed for bed and arose the next morning as daylight came. Artificial light has changed all that. Because of unlimited access to light and how freely it is used, the current tendency is for people to be out of sync with their natural internal clock. There are simple things that can be done to entrain with the internal clock again and have restorative sleep.

DIMMING THE LIGHT

During the day, the more natural, outside light you can experience, the more your body will be ready to go to sleep at night. During the evening as night approaches, it helps to aid the readiness to sleep if the lights become dimmer.

If there are especially bright lights in the house, they could be turned off or dimmed. Incandescent lights are more helpful in prepping for sleep than LEDs or fluorescent. This is a good time for Himalayan salt lamps or candlelight.

WINDING DOWN

Natural daylight contains a lot of blue light. Electronic lighted devices also emit blue light. This kind of light works for daytime but is disruptive for sleep if it is experienced during the hours of preparation leading up to bedtime or at night. It is helpful to prepare for sleep by tapering off of TV, the computer and other lighted devices as the evening progresses. No lighted devices an hour before bedtime.

If lighted devices are used before bedtime, the possible unwanted effects on sleeping can be minimized by wearing blue light blocking glasses. They could be worn if you simply have to use lighted devices in the evening or choose to watch TV. Yes, these orangey, amber colored glasses change the way everything looks. It can be worth it though, because by wearing them to block blue light, you have a chance to be sleeping well all night.

If you use a computer during the evening, another thing that can help is to download a program which, during the evening and on through the night, blocks a good deal of the blue light your computer screen emits. The next morning, the computer automatically resets to the normal kind of lighted screen. Here is a site you can visit for a free download, f.lux. A good download for pay site is Iris.

SUPPLEMENTS

There is a trio of supplements when taken 20 to 30 minutes or more before bedtime is super effective for promoting excellent sleep. Take as directed.

* 5-HTP containing added small amounts of B6 and C
* Magnesium Malate
* Melatonin

There are a number of different kinds of magnesium. Whichever one you choose, use powdered capsule form delivery in the body. Follow the dosage recommen... magnesium than your body wants, it will tell you. The magnesium ... secreted through the colon. You can then back off the dosage.

Just a note: If you experience leg cramps in the night, taking a capsule of magnesium can most likely take care of it quickly.

Select a natural, plant-based, vegetarian formula of melatonin. If you are taking a liquid form of melatonin, drop the dosage onto a spoon and lick it off with the underside of the tongue. This will allow the body to absorb it quickly.

If you are taking drugs or supplements at bedtime, check with your physician or health practitioner to see if there is another time they could be taken. Many drugs and supplements are stimulating. That is the last thing you want this time in the evening.

Also check with your health care practitioner to see if the above sleep enhancing supplements would be compatible with whatever you may be taking, either during the day or in the evening, whether it is drugs or supplements. Some supplements are not compatible with each other.

TUB SOAK

An incredibly easy and delightful way to unwind and relax is to take a tub soak using hot water, sea salt and baking soda. About a cup each of sea salt and baking soda should do it. It doesn't have to be measured out carefully. Use more if you want. This is a really simple and enjoyable way to let go of tensions and get ready for going to bed.

If you do not have a water purification system where you live, add to the tub soak 1,000 mg of the ascorbic acid form of vitamin C. Use the powdered form. A tablet doesn't dissolve quickly. A tablet could be crushed, of course, if you wanted to take the time, but the powder is quick and easy. The ascorbic acid neutralizes the chlorine in the water and makes it a healthier soak. Add it while the tub is filling so it will be distributed through all the water by the time the tub is filled and ready for you.

GRATITUDE

During the time of preparation for bed, one of the most beneficial things you can do to prepare your brain and mind for sleep is to think about things you are grateful for. No matter what is happening in your life, or not, there are always many things to be thankful for. It can also be a powerfully good habit to write these things down.

Scientific studies have shown being grateful is a way to increase happiness and satisfaction with your life. The studies also indicate having gratitude benefits your physical health in dozens of ways. Go ahead, make a list. It's good medicine. Natural, the best.

CHAPTER 4

Going to Bed

"Before you sleep, read something that is
exquisite and worth remembering."

— DESIDERIUS ERASMUS

THE DAY IS COMING TO a close. The thoughtful and deliberate preparing for sleep you have done during the day and through the evening is paying off now in a big way.

TIMING FOR BEDTIME

Humans are creatures of habit. Creating a new habit by deliberately changing your way of preparing for sleep can be life changing in an awesome way. For the purpose of consistently sleeping well, it is important to go to bed at about the same time every night.

Some people like to go to bed early and rise early. Others tend to want to go to bed later and get up later. Part of what will dictate when you go to bed is the time you have to get up the next morning to get ready for work or to take care of your family's needs. Just have the intention to be consistent.

Whatever time you choose to go to bed, it might be good if you can be asleep by at least 11:00 pm. The body does a major amount of recharging between 11:00 pm and 1:00 am, so it is in your best interest to cooperate with this natural cycle.

The average time of sleep that seems to be supportive of health and good functioning in our society today is seven to nine hours. Some people seem to do fine with less than seven. You probably know where you fit into this picture.

SLEEPWEAR

If you choose to use sleepwear at night, select things that are made of natural fiber. Take your pick from cotton, linen, silk, hemp, bamboo or wool. Organic would be the best. It is wonderfully comfortable to wear nightclothes made of cotton t-shirt material, especially if they are loose fitting.

It is sleep enhancing to wear socks at night during the cool/cold seasons. Loose, cotton or wool socks are the best. If the socks you are going to be wearing at night have a tight, elastic ribbing at the top, cut it off. It is important to have good circulation in your legs and feet as you sleep.

FINAL BEDTIME RITUALS

Reading something that inspires you right before going to bed is an important piece of the puzzle (no reading in bed). It can be productive for going to sleep quickly to have already done the physical preparation for bedtime before you start reading. Flossing and brushing your teeth, bathing—if that is your regular time for a shower or bath, dressing for bed.

This would be a good time to apply a drop or two of lavender essential oil to your wrists or the bone behind your ears. Lavender essential oil is well known for its ability to help relax the body. It is often used at bedtime to assist in falling off to sleep. The essential oil needs to be a pure form—no chemicals added. Using an essential oil containing chemicals would be a major detractor from healthful sleep.

INSPIRATIONAL READING

The importance and effectiveness of this stage of preparing for sleep cannot be over stated. Choose to read whatever inspires you and lifts you to a higher state of mind, whatever makes you feel good. If it involves your heart as well as your mind, more the better. The body responds incredibly well to this activity.

Read a while, then put the book down and walk straight to bed, maybe only stopping to turn down the thermostat and visit the bathroom. This final bedtime protocol of getting ready for bed and then reading last of all can greatly facilitate easing into sleep quickly and easily. It sounds like a little bit of nothing type tip, but it works really well. It is a big one.

Once you reach a high, pleasant state of gratitude and inspiration, you can almost be floating as you walk to bed.

GOING TO BED

As you enter the bedroom, close the door behind you to maintain the darkness. Have the flashlight handy, the one that is emitting an orange light, if you need it to navigate to your bed in the highly darkened room.

CHAPTER 5

Slipping into Sleeping

"The best cure for insomnia is to get a lot of sleep."

— W. C. FIELDS

BECAUSE OF ALL THE STEPS you have taken during the day and evening to have a good sleep tonight, you just might fall right off to sleep a few seconds after your head touches the pillow. If it has been an extra stimulating day, you may be able to use a little more help to go off to dreamland. There are some easy physical and then also mental things you can pick and choose from to aid in dropping off to sleep now.

STROKING YOUR HANDS AND ARMS

It can be immensely reassuring and relaxing to gently stroke your hands and arms. With this simple movement, feelings of reassurance, well-being and relaxation can arise from deep in the brain. It only takes a few seconds to get awesome results. This technique also works well during the day when you feel stressed or uptight or if you just need a short break.

SLEEPING WITH A COVER

When your body was developing in the womb, you were experiencing constant pressure on your skin. It may be helpful to slightly mimic this by always sleeping with a cover of some sort. In the warm/hot months, it could be as little as a light sheet. It can help to have a deeper, more constant sleep. Could it be that this small amount of pressure on your body triggers early primal memories that have a comforting effect?

If this works well and you are willing to experiment, the next step would be to sleep with a weighted cover. This kind of product is available as a sheet, a blanket or a comforter. Start with a low weight—4 or 5 pounds to begin with. This amount of weight might ultimately be heavy enough to get the desired results. The weighted covers are available up to 25 pounds.

Choose a cover smaller than the size of your mattress to minimize the possibility of it sliding off your bed as you sleep.

STRETCHING YOUR LEGS

This tip is for side sleepers only.

There sometimes is the tendency to bend your legs when you are lying in bed, ready to go off to sleep. There may be times when you find yourself almost in a fetal position. It may be more productive to stretch them out, almost straight. There is a pronounced difference in the quality of body energy it is possible to experience in each of these two positions of the legs, bent or straight.

The purpose of acupuncture is to assist the body to have more freely flowing energy. When an acupuncturist inserts the needles, the energy they are manipulating is called "chi" (chee). This chi can flow through the body more freely when the legs are straightened out than when they are bent. You may be able to notice this difference if you try each position for a few seconds. Freer flow of chi equals better sleep.

BALANCING YOUR BODY

Place your pointer fingers on your neck, just under your earlobes, beside your jawbones. One finger on each side, right finger on the right side and left finger on the left side. Using just a light, gentle touch, hold this position for a minute or two or as long as you choose to.

You may notice a pulse in each of your fingers. (If you don't feel a pulse, not to worry.) This is not a vascular pulse, but most likely a pulse in the bioenergetic field of the body. If you can feel the pulse, you may notice each finger is pulsing at a different rate and rhythm. After a while, the pulses will come into sync. At this point, you no longer need to continue holding these places on your neck. This is effective for assisting in balancing the energy of the body and for better alignment of the spine, especially the neck area.

ONE OF THE ULTIMATE SLEEP HACKS

If you are anywhere near going to sleep, this just may put you over.

This can work whether you are a side sleeper or a back sleeper.

Take hold of some hair on the back of your head and gently pull up, slightly tucking your chin, all in the same movement. At the same time, scoot your hips down, away from the trunk of your body. The amount of movement you are creating could be measured as a fraction of an inch. This is a small but significant movement.

If you do not have hair on the back of your head, open one hand, place it on the back of your head and pull upward as you move the hips away from the trunk. Easily, gently.

The reason this slight shift works is that it can allow a better flow of blood and cerebrospinal fluid to the brain.

CLOSED MOUTH BREATHING

The nose is for breathing, the mouth is for eating.

This is especially true for sleeping. Mouth breathing is mostly for the normal, everyday purposes of talking and eating. Otherwise, it is healthier to keep the mouth closed. Nose breathing gets better levels of oxygen to organs and tissues of the body. The ratio between oxygen and CO_2 in the lungs is more normal.

Breathing through the mouth during the night can cause dehydration. That, of course, could precipitate waking up, getting up to get a drink of water. Mouth breathers often have bad breath. Tooth decay and gum disease can result from mouth breathing. People who have asthma or sleep apnea are often mouth breathers.

If you are a mouth breather, practice keeping your mouth closed during the day. At night, use a one-inch strip of surgical tape over your mouth. If you cannot keep it on all night, continue to use the tape until you can or until you can nose breathe all night.

Slow, easy, natural breathing through the nose can calm you and help initiate sleep.

AWARENESS OF YOUR BREATH

As you lie in bed, sense the in and out movement of your breath. Notice how the air going into your nose is cool, and the air coming out is warm—all in the same breath. Feel the gentle rising and falling of your chest. Give attention to how your diaphragm, the midsection area, is moving as you breathe.

If your mind wanders from this phenomenon of watching your breathing, gently bring it back once you realize your attention has drifted off. It, of course, is a normal thing for the mind to shift from one thing to another of its own accord.

When you concentrate on the breath, the rate of breathing will tend to change even if you are not trying to alter the rhythm of it. Just continue to bring your focus back to your breath. Let the breathing happen.

SOUND IN YOUR THROAT

You have heard the saying, "Don't try this at home." For this application, it changes to "Don't try this if you are sleeping in the same room with someone."

Here goes. With your mouth closed, make a sound in your throat at the back of your tongue as you breathe in and also on the out breath. It is not exactly the most beautiful sound ever. It does, however, sharpen the focus on the breath. It also has the plus of naturally slowing down the rate of breathing. Breathing more slowly can be a factor in relaxing the body.

HOLDING A FINGER

The sensation of being held can be relaxing, reassuring and balancing. With one hand, lightly hold a finger on the other hand, any finger. Hold it for as long or as little as you want. Shift to a different finger for a bit if you have the urge to.

This little activity can also be used during the day. It works well if you are in a meeting or lecture. No one will notice.

HOLDING YOUR THUMBS

Here is another holding type relaxation technique to slip into sleep. (If holding a finger in a lying down position is not perfectly comfortable for you, this position will be.)

Make a light fist with both hands. On each hand, place your thumbs between your first two fingers. It is possible to have the relaxing and reassuring feeling with this configuration and also to have more freedom of movement and more choices of body position than with the Holding a Finger suggestion.

POSITIONING THE TONGUE

Placing the tongue on the roof of the mouth with the tip of the tongue touching the upper teeth will create balance in the flow of chi in the body, which assists in relaxing. To find the exact position of the tongue that is optimal, say the word "low." When you pronounce the "l," your tongue is in exactly the right place to create the balance and relaxation you are looking to achieve.

BEING GRATEFUL

If your mind starts spinning with thoughts of worry or anxiety, gratitude is a great antidote. Think about your day. Think of each of the positive things that happened to you. There will be quite a list. There always is. No matter what direction your life takes, there are always plenty of things to be thankful for.

When you start thinking about the good in your life, it's like finding a sweet spot. The energy in your body shifts and becomes lighter and freer. An inner smile shows up. Something in you says, "Thank you. Yes, I can do this. I can keep going and do my best." It's a good space to be in as you drift off to sleep.

COUNTING (NOT SHEEP)

Count backwards from one hundred by sevens.

Still awake?

Count backwards from one hundred by seven and nine sixteenths. That should do it. Night, night.

IMAGINE SLEEPING

"See" yourself in the most pleasant setting possible, sleeping peacefully. Use your imagination to the fullest. The sky is the limit. Visualize the smallest details. Feel the peace of this picture of ideal sleep. Sometimes that is when sleep slips in.

YOUR NAME

On your way to sleep, silently repeat your name over and over. Your own name is one of the most special words in your vocabulary. Mentally saying your name at nighttime in bed is as if you are calling yourself into a state of sleep.

CHAPTER 6

The Next Morning

"Sleep is the golden chain that ties health and our bodies together."

— THOMAS DEKKER

IT IS A GREAT GIFT when you wake up in the morning and one of the first realizations is that you have slept well all night long. What a way to start the day.

The changes you made to get a good night of sleep are well worth it. Immeasurably valuable, actually. Quality sleep is essential to good health.

If you can work it in, spending a few minutes outside in the sun or at a sunlit window will give you a kick-start as you begin the day. The bright, natural, blue light of the sun supports your light/dark circadian rhythm to shift from the dark mode to the light side of the cycle.

Have a good day, the best ever.